GALDR

thought + memory

MICHAEL RAVEN

Raw Earth Ink

2022

This book is a work of poetry.

First paperback edition March 2022

Cover art by Ash Halloran
Book design by tara caribou

ISBN 979-8-98504-063-0 (paperback)

Published by Raw Earth Ink
PO Box 39332
Ninilchik, AK 99639
www.taracaribou.com

Dedicated to all the broken things, seers and shamen, the misfits, and the lost. Most of all, this work is dedicated to my fylgja, which has never left my side, although I have given plenty of reasons for them to leave.

May all of you find your way safely home.

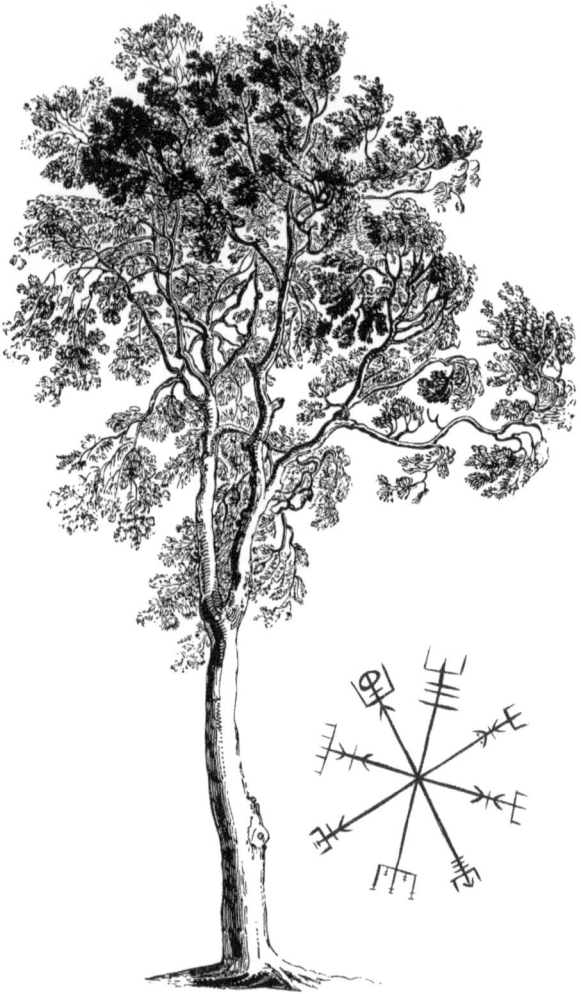

tik-tock

tik-tock
the time slipstreams
caught inside the maelstrom
two ravens whispering
present and past
but never tomorrow because –
tomorrow never knows

old grim, one-eyed
drinks to you health and hearth
knowing you'll dance on air
in the forever night
singing songs only shadows know
if only to escape the storm

tik-tock
midnight's kiss
growing cold on pale lips

autumn roads

weary roads followed
autumn wayside rests
call my fatigued soul
promising an eternity
of sleep under a
blanket of orange
and red leaves

z

lost between the sheets
we gorged ourselves on slumber
while drunk from flesh on flesh
while winter raged darkly outside
a chill kissing bare skin through
single-pane windows
& cracked caulking

temptations

essence drained
i miss the skinfringe numbness
whiskey used to bring with
comfortflask warmth
coursing through my
arthritic heart
easing stilted seizured
staccatotaut beats
no whispering down phones
like a song's razorscut
singing will you still hold
me tonight? mutterwise slideways
shut the vault to amber Gold
calling colliding with
desire untamed unquenched
fire staved off with
mocktails empty abscess

only
the hunger, i know
will remain

so
i writhe numbless
tonight
again

mankato

laughing naked
between sheets
marked with love bites
and bruises
entwined –
shades and fugues
a phantasm of you

library

secret shoe dangle
high arch
i pretend focus
on leather-bound books

anamnesis

craving the
love bites and
bruises your mouth
leaves behind

close

was that you
kissing the dream?
street children giggled
shyly behind dirty hands

re | life

what is the purpose
in living so many lives
if we never touch again?
i dig into the spirits' soil
muddied to squeeze answers straight
a raven behind says,
you ask the wrong question;
only time will tell

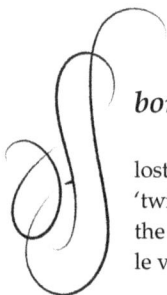

borderlands

lost in the borderlands
'twixt stocking, soft thigh –
the night garden,
le val sans retour

sirens

today
i am brim-filled with mistrust
of anyone, anything
and, especially: myself
overflowing with black doubts
every word, every thought
obfuscating fogs of mendacity
is there any honesty at all?

i recall –
maudlin and drunk, i could hear
all of those sweet fucking lies
and not give a shit at all

it is the numbness i miss most
that lethe-loving driftwood
sensation and i slipstreamed
through my stupid life

the bottle calls on days like this
a siren song promising to
drown out caring about
truth, dare, or deceit
it promises comfort
in a turbulent sea
that threatens to
smash me against
dark razorblade rocks

transmissions

old haunts night restless
an unexpected séance
with their unclear messages
failing to come through
       ethereal byways

those
       whispers without mediums?
           how do you capture
           emotion without
           an ouija,
    without planchette rattling
squeaking
   over styled gothic lettering?

i don't know
           i don't know
once said
           someone
   i used to know

   carmine splashed spirit boards

     – is that of heaven?

calliope (summer wine)

slumber with me
like lazy summer wine
stolen kisses along
your thighs and sighs
dewdrop drunk on
your ambrosia
and the time
becomes meaningless
there are only
eternal moments
of you, you, and you
and who gives a damn
about tomorrow?
or yesterday?
when your fingers
trace my spine
and i drink you
like lazy summer wine

path to perdition

i am burning
a tincture of acid
a demitasse of flame
pouring though me

i am burning
my feet held to the edge
of hell's outer doors
sulfur choking madness

this immolation is self-inflicted
writhing punishment
these hot whips i conjured
for daemons' delight

how they laugh at my agony!

the illusions are tempting
seductive, desirable
but
    just
        out
           of
               [REACH]
    i am my own
succubus

Michael Raven

enchanting my mind with
self-made promises and whimsy
seeing pouts and sultry eyes
where lips and oculus stand

you lech...

fingers burn eyes blaze
the heat
          the heat
pulling back from the precipice
aching for a gracious stranger
to sooth the flame with
a touch a turning word
spell my relief

but
sanctuary doesn't come
and so...

i shuffle to my cell and ask
my torturer to dream me
another dose of pain
in the three o'clock hour
          wondering when
the heart attack will
                    spawn

sanctuary

lost highways trailing
off into the night
left of the dial singing
she sells sanctuary

the world drags me down...

and the flurries dancing
headlight swaying
fairies in the sky
your hand on the shift-stick
and my eyes upon
your smile

the fire in your eyes keeps me...

fields of grain standing
winter blurring on the side
too late, too late
the fishnet you wear
can't keep them alive
lady
lady
lay

the sparkle in your eyes keeps...

and the wolves
they howl as your hand
steals away into mine
faux leopard print
you lean to me
eyes still on the lights
the road the night
a kiss leaving me sighing
and dying

inside her you'll find sanctuary
inside her you'll find...

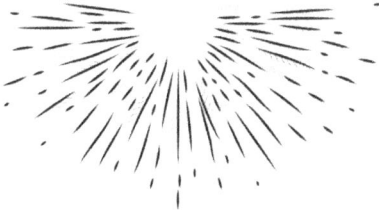

horsemen

i am pain

∴

syringe injected acid rust
corrupt rotten meat
distended joint gristle
shrieking banshee howls
rubbed raw on river rock
frenzy liquored gangrene

and poison

that too

∴

there is no sleep
only wakeful slumber
segue slide to opaque scrim
the cards shuffle shuffle shuffle
those manic birds overhead
recalling my sins

just
in case i forgot

oh, moonbeam
why me?

∴

leaden in the belly
i navigate my corpses again
my own sad moment
in the role of sisyphus
with shame my stone
the third time
perhaps?
perhaps?
per–

projections

the veil is thin
tonight | | tonight
i think i might
lose my way
wandering foggy
moor paths
rock filled, knives
were it not for
anchoring lace knots
tied to many
possible pasts
carried buried
safe within my chest
blooded with the
midnight trains
never made &
lovers lost
in darkest shadows
night

otherworld stalking
i will-o-wisp
alight & thither where...
ça et là
& everywhen between
ghosting through the murk
i kissed you in passing
do my lips still burn
on your full, lush breast?
i saw you there:
standing
dreaming
a secret smile
lingering
before
i drift
silent & home

sgàthach

tainted by geis
to never know her touch beyond
the shadows night, shades, ghosts
i kiss velvet petals, eyes closed
envisioning full, moist lips
before the winds carry them away

queen anne

that lingering dream –
as absurd as it may be –
i think it was you
looking over
your shoulder
with a wink
and a smile
dawn atop
queen anne hill
fog clinging
to your legs
as if children spelled
to their mother
all
white ribbons
smoky lace
before the ravens
exploded
the sky with
their raucous
tok tok toks:
this this this
they cried

station

i like to pretend
it is you, there,
at the station
waiting in your
sensible black dress with
sensible black shoes
your dark hair
a jumble of curls
for my train to
come in

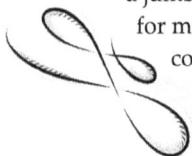

Michael Raven

hedge

eyes
  eyes
    eyes
watching quiet
for signs
  ley lines
  leading to
another's
  designs
in the
  labyrinth
  a path to
the heart of
  soul of
    mind of
    the mad
    troubadour
lost in silent
hedges broken
      and
forlorn

don't ask silly questions

raven dancing on
a beach of stone
croaking
change change change

i asked why
it could never stay
the same
even if just a
short while
and she laughed,
the sound of
rending rust

ha ha ha

pasteries of romance

i recall the snow falling
impossibly large flakes while
waiting for hamlet to
mime madness &
ophelia to slip under the waters

you offered me a
poppyseed-filled pastry
your mother had made
like a fool, i turned it down

you frowned

years later, you laughed
said i was just
hopeless romantic
when i said
i still loved you

i blame
my refusal of
that pastry
for my loss

no more heroes

world weary
empathic
train wreck
in a plague of
chronic mistrust

no more heroes
no desire remains
fatigued with all
this poison
oozing from
those festering
wounds

nightwash

underwater flowing
over silt and stone
rub skin, stream wash
rub mud, you and me
make land, this flesh
make river, this blood
rub wash, stream skin
rub silt, me and you

can't you hear them crying?
can't you hear their scream?
flesh and blood and silt and stream
spirits in the night –

phantasmagoria

wraith remembrances
of phantom pasts haunt
me, each clinging like
gossamer filigree
to entwine me to the
desolation of worlds
without end

pulled through the harrow
scraped clear of all hope
the taunting begins anew
chimaerical hands
reaching with fresh promises
for fools

solstice

night's cold finger darkness
lingers on your spine, old jack
dancing icewater
turned glass backbone
as you slide through
thin-ice cracks, glide-skating
waiting for the slow-dawn rising

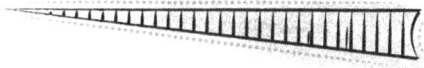

skinwalking

i am the
black-footed
fox
prowling your
sleepless nights
leaving a trail
of footprints
in that winter
place

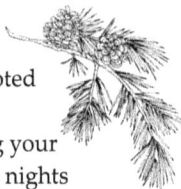

unkindness

crimson on obsidian
scarlet on tourmaline
paint me blood black
on virgin white snow
feathers scattered
stained vermilion in
the ruby sunset glow
the toc-toc-toc fading
in the distance with
the rifle report

mists

the veils stretch thin
in this morning's
humid haze
drawing to
hidden places
'twixt and 'tween
i will follow
i say
but the worlds
fade
away
with the lance-pierce
ray of sun

time a time folding
back becoming the
river barge threads
needle eyes
every night, flowing
death standing
the stern
with a wink

this is the sea

unmoored and adrift
i reach out for two hands
to plunge me into icy waters
delve into my felon chest
to draw the poison of
forever years from my soul
black burnt pitch thick
with coagulated blood pudding

draw out the fetid fantasies
draw out the traitorous dreams
tear out the scarred soul meat
and
  and
    kill off the pale, sick-filled me

this dying is necessary
    the vessel, cleared and
        the soul filled with the
    the ever-moving sea

horizons draw eyes
    for this is the sea

good night, though

in the shadowlands
and their loathsome lonely
i talk to ghosts who
with nothing much to say
they nod and murmur
grow distant, fade
away away away
their talk, idle stuff
small talk soliloquy
lacking depth, substance
phantom words from
phantom mouths
and, like the ash in the plains
weightless, choking
and tastelessly crisp
lost paper dolls
at the forever party
doldrums

threads; bare

bound
constrained
clockwork springs
tick tock things
winding
tying
b
i
t
i
n
g
into my....
spirit rhymes
tearing into....
my sagging skin

flesh within flesh within meat within
me
threads broken
under the strain
and tangle-tossed
heap

hunted

peel back skin layers me
exposing the nerves
electric sparking
exsanguinate & rejuvenate
& fill the spirit we
nightlong howling for
growing is change is pain
or
meaningless
meaning less
then
leave this fresh dressed
kill hanging me
to age into essence
whiskey leather
and sinew

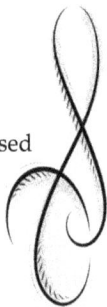

the river

the river
       runs down
washing
  the dirt
the stains
from me
       the scars
   that shroud
       the scars
lacerating
my mind
my flesh
    that cut into
          me
        me
      me

.

ᚨᛗᛁᛏ

slow unfurling
twirling the ribbon
rags unfixed threads turning
crosswebs tangled
drifting across
tangled yarns tighten
fast hung and pierced
with thorns septic
swaying in the winds
in the tree, in the nines
and the waves wash fast
with the spirits of mine
over and spill brim
eye turned grim
a girl singing single
her songs

born to this
borne of this
the gallows hanging horde
wolves, they howl
unkindness laughing at
my eye
my eye my
eye
i lost my i

watching for
the mystery reveal

cast out the drauger dregs
and fill those toothsome
carvings blood
i am hanging here tonight
high above your
serpent's throne

someone take these dreams away
sang the rock shaman
of our day
reversed, I sing the same
tortured by the swaying
of the branches
from which
i hang

urðr galdr

shadowed –
i look to mother moon
for her cold comfort to
chill this burning ache
throbbing so in my chest
i think i may have been
dreaming too hard
under her bright
autumn light

lunacy, some might say

and
perhaps...

perhaps
they are
right

spellbound:
is this ~~aptrburdhr~~ rebirth
cast in the cloth of
you me and these?
because this is what
i dreamt
hanging under the
gallows tree

i would shed an eye
for the eternal you
to know those mysteries
those things
merely misplaced
if my dreaming was
true

forge

the sigils and signs
hard and firm
hammer me into shape
sending sparks
showering the ground

i will be remade
– willing or not

surrender is the easy path

weapon or tool?
the shape of things to come
is still not evident
in the burning red heat
of potential

it is not my decision
i can choose my path
but not the fate
the destiny
each forging beats
me to submission

i finally submit

reflections

words
deadwood
focused on rite
trope & tilt of earth

i want
soulrend
heartburst
mindbleed
musclestrain
star explosions
filling wholly
the cosmic me
climbing the
eternal tree

thought+memory

i walk my own path
through the woods
with wights clinging
to my side
– they remain
silent
watchful,
waiting for the dim one
to learn how
to speak their tongue

phantom passing touches
of strangers give slight
warmth, but
never ever enough
& the mists
always return to
chilling flesh, bone, heart

they hop:
branch to branch to
ground to stump to rot
sometimes laughing
at the fool following
sometimes chiding
the child who is following

Michael Raven

sometimes silently
guiding the man wandering
down the narrow
wooded path
– memory escaping
– thought deepening
while the trees backfill
the footprinted loam
behind

ways

the new ways lie broken
shattered and painted in
dried blood stigmata
the culling of overgrowth
ignored

the groves return
old growth, old ways, old songs
where honor still lives
fathered by ash
oak thorn

we sold souls for tuppence
where we should have
kept the gold
hold on to the old ways
hold on to before

gambled lives
gambled lies
time to toss the dice &
watch the bones dance
before settling the score

blinding

with blind bound eyes
i might see those
threads trailing
like gossamer
dancing in the wind

restless

night fall
and the ghosts
filter in and
sit next to me
in the dark
accusatory and
impatient
staring until
the stories
start again

farceur

blackwing dizzy dance
widdershins in rain
heyoka, hey blackwing
bloodkissed, moonkissed
trickster, shaman
no – fool

blackwing dizzy dance
playing in the rain

peril

i darksee the hurt share we
tattoo blood smeared me
painted for war
barbs, burrs and
busted glass words
gnawed for bloodsport

tangled in snares and
dawnrazor light scythes
crawling
crawling
in the mud towards
a *more*
painless oblivion

myhandyourhand
CLASPED
drag on me
through the wastelands we
to another fractish place

evermore it seems
this muddy plain
leechsucks the marrow
cold and harrow
ribbonstreams
damned, i am
but you...
might be set free

hands etherslip
see
SEE

warded

bury these wishes at
the old oak tree
wait for them to grow
and take root
but
   they will not,
            will they?
wishes are wishes and
i cannot stop wishing
damned to disappointment
i claw back dirt
and i
    and i
       and i
         and i
bury the wishes deep
inside the locks around
my
          heart

toktoktok

my zen practice is
that of a drunken raven
shouting vulgarities
at the wind

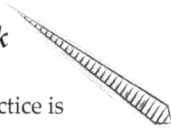

driromancy

what garbage,
these words i write –
better to chew razors
and spit blood out
in patterns
to read
as if
telling
fortunes

 ***splinter***

like the cold hard rain
i dash myself against
the stones & splinter

slip

sometimes,
she said, an ocean weight intoned
you forget the how of tears
she laid down her book
of poems,
ghosted away with
winter in her wake

Michael Raven

cyanide

press a thorn
a thorn a dagger
a dagger to my throat

pinprick
blood
wells
symphony

tie me up &
tie me down
mock the sad-faced
gothic clown

needles
are
the release
for me

net capture
the killing jar & cyanide
pin & needle
pin & needle

put
me
up high on
your shelf

i hate words

i toss these words on
the walls like the shit
that they are
i love words, i hate words
it's like trying to paint the sky
when all you have for paint
is green and even when there's blue
it is the **wrong shade** of blue
rubbish, tripe and crap
all...

hand me your flowery words
fifty cents a piece
and i shit on them too
there should be no-thought
no-think – just

an immature wind
playing through onyx curls
on a sunny day in amber fields
of tall grass waving to the sky
her smile she doesn't know
she wears, and even in the smudge
of grass and soil betraying
the kisses she stole
and swallowed whole

words...
words never capture that
quite right

queries

twist the fountain pen
bleed some ink spill it like
a spatterpunk novel over
skullcap reams
lockpicking secret diaries
i keep hidden from myself
what do i mean?
are the words not clear?

no

that's because the
wraiths hunt in
the winter places
deep within
a place even i dare not tread
because
 – it is
        unquestionably uglier
              in that dank place
              that i can convey
we don't open this door
no one is allowed here
said the butler to the fly
ignore the man behind the curtain
he is only a lie

desire stalks the street
high on the bile
axeblades honey dripping words
killer killer killer
who will love him tomorrow?

the taste of ash-infused
lacrima across my cheek
will the buckthorn serve tonight?

what words? these are not words?
these are hell freshened with barbed wire
this is love

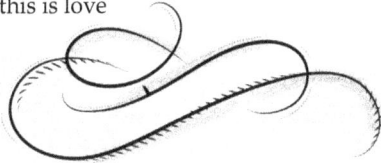

words

i need words so old
they are new
the ones i have are
abused and confused and
quite often misused

i need a word in the
language of rain
sunlight green in the grey
pouring though to the ground
and that sound
pounding, pummeling wet
the pavement in spring

a secret told by the wind
through and to trees sighing
with heavy breaths
in the oak and the pine and
the cottonwood shaking
even the lone crow herald
telling where the murder began

a story of night
a fable of day
the night stars passing on wisdom
as stardust
lost relatives on the edge of sky

give me no signs no symbols
give me no half-shadowed lies
i need words
beyond words...

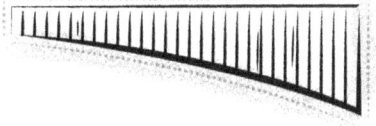

nursery play

grindylow grabkin from the marl-pit you
rawhead and bloodybones, they feast on you
shake you shape you like so much meat
grindylow and bloodybones will eat your feet

Michael Raven

on the wing

the raven queen
tattoos me with her
dreamtime kiss
that still lingers
bittersweet
    after i
        wake

lost in the flatlands

missing my youth
with the trysting
music without rules
and fuck all attitudes

cigarettes
that not drunk buzz
exchanging glances
playing in a band
and waking at noon

all gone now...
just aches and pains and worries
with looks faded like
worn out jeans

melancholy

memories –
seasoned w/ crooked smiles
& tristesse

melrose

there, the killing fields fallow
grey stones above stumble-tumbling
in a slow march back to ground
rain-speckled cold paints names
ravaged by wind and time
gargoyles hang there, too

listen to the silence –
sidhe still sing in the empty places
the hollow spaces between
for a king long given to dust

i follow their procession
ghosts of the fire-ravaged lost
as they shamble towards a god
who abandoned them there
the swell of the choir and
light shafts from the rain
remembrances

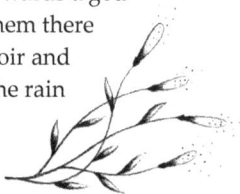

vogue, saturday nights

we stood like whores
as we waited for ascension
caring, not caring
if we were found desirable.
hot sweat flowing
the scent of libido
burning in our noses
music, our religion
sent the soul a-thrumming
looking, not looking
hoping for a star
needing
some kind of stranger
to fall into our
arms

about the author

MICHAEL RAVEN has been murdering innocent words since some time in primary school and hasn't had the decency to stop after he was first published in second grade. He is an equal-opportunity destroyer of words, having written not only poetry, but fiction, technical papers, philosophical and neopagan essays, as well as being the primary lyricist for bands playing music ranging from punk to old school gothic to Irish-inspired folk. In the mid-90s, he was the emcee and primary organizer (with the extensive help of several partners) in a spoken word/open mic salon, *Sweet Immolation*, located in Seattle's Belltown neighborhood.

Since that time, Michael has become more reclusive and has focused primarily on quietly exploring ecstatic and shamanic approaches towards verse – poetry often based in Taoist,

Zen, Native American and Northern European traditions (Celtic and Norse).

Michael currently resides in the suburbs of the Minneapolis/Saint Paul area with too many cats. He wouldn't mind returning to the NW Coast and opening an espresso bar when he retires so he can try to make the philosopher's stone equivalent of the perfect shot of espresso.